The Mammoth Cave has caves at five different levels and covers nearly 500 square kilometres.

Did you know that ...

... the Mammoth Cave in Kentucky in the USA is the biggest cave system in the world?

Limestone caves

Limestone is a hard, grey rock. When rain falls on limestone, the water goes through cracks in the rock. Rainwater can dissolve limestone.

Very slowly, the limestone dissolves along the cracks. After thousands of years, holes and tunnels form in the rock and they get bigger and bigger until a cave appears.

Did you know that ...

... most caves are limestone caves?

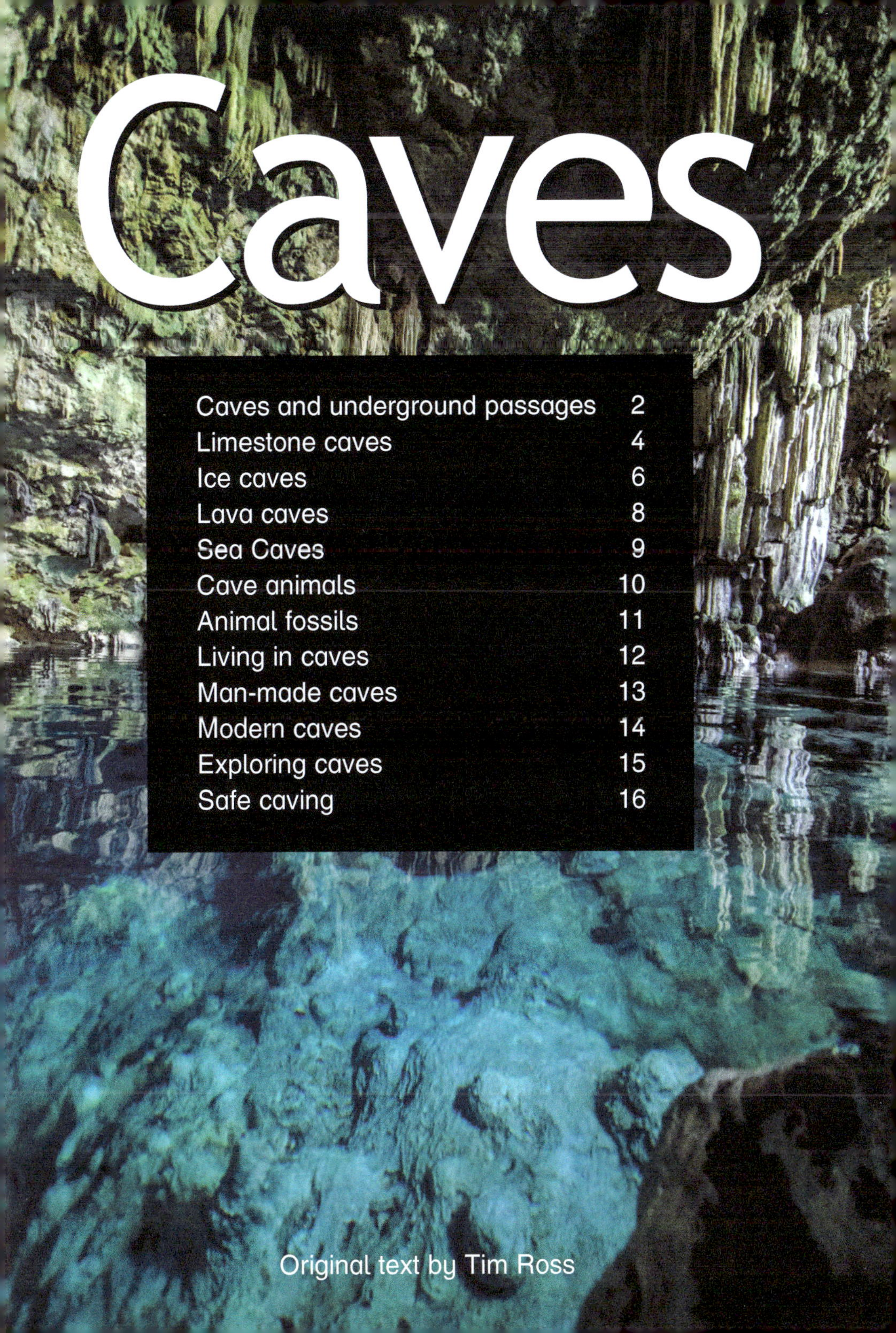

Caves

Original text by Tim Ross

Caves and underground passages

Caves are hollow spaces in rock or ice. Some caves are smaller than a room in a house; others are enormous.

The system of passages that connects a group of caves can be as big as a city. Sometimes passages and tunnels are hundreds of kilometres long. Sometimes underground rivers go through the caves and form underground lakes.

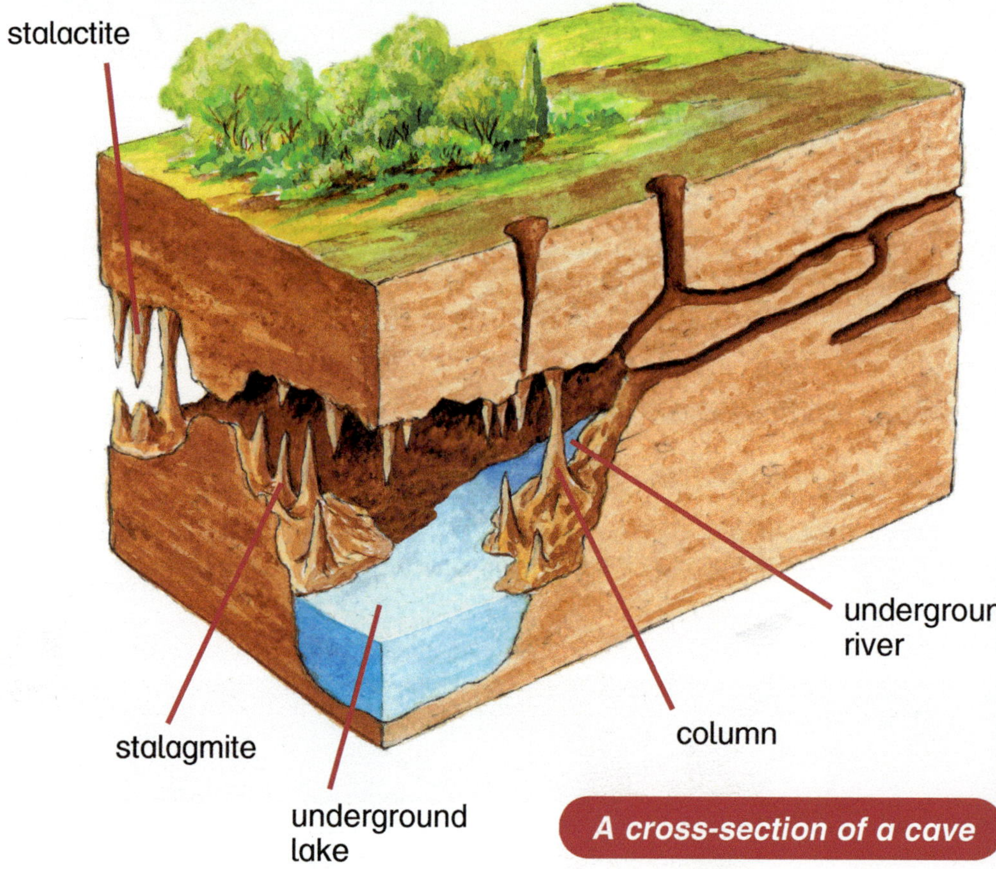

A cross-section of a cave

Limestone caves sometimes have amazing rock formations. Some look like giant candles or tall chimneys.

Stalactites grow down from the roof of the cave. *Stalagmites* grow up from the floor of the cave. Sometimes after thousands and thousands of years, a stalagmite and stalactite meet and then form a solid column of rock.

Did you know that ...

... it can take one year for a stalactite to grow 2 centimetres?

Ice caves

Ice caves often appear under glaciers. Glaciers are enormous mountains of ice which move very, very slowly. Sometimes warm air and water under the glacier help the ice to melt and make an ice cave. The ice caves do not exist for long.

An ice cave in a glacier

Ice caves can also appear inside rock caves. The water on the walls of the cave turns into ice. The ice covers the walls of the cave like a big refrigerator.

Did you know that ...

... ice caves are the most dangerous kinds of cave?

Lava caves

Lava caves sometimes appear when a volcano erupts. Red-hot lava flows from the volcano and makes a river of lava. The outside of the river of lava cools down and changes into solid rock. But inside, the lava is still moving and it travels along the inside of the rock tube. When there is no more hot lava, there is an empty, hollow tube. This is a lava cave.

Did you know that ...

... the longest lava cave is in Hawaii and is more than 11 kilometres long?

Sea caves

Waves crash against the soft rocks of cliffs and form sea caves.

This sea cave has formed in a cliff.

Cave animals

Caves are very difficult places to survive. There is no light and there are no plants. But there are animals that live in caves. There are eels, spiders, scorpions, bats and insects. Sometimes bears sleep all winter in caves.

One of the strangest cave animals is a blind fish which lives in the Ozark caves in Oklahoma in the USA. The fish has no eyes and no colour. There is no light in the rivers and lakes where it lives, so the fish swims in total darkness.

Did you know that ...

... as many as 200,000 bats live in the huge bat colony in the Carlsbad caves in the USA?

Animal fossils

Caves can give us important information about the past. In 2002 in Western Australia there was an important discovery – a cave with perfect fossil skeletons.

All the fossil skeletons were from enormous animals which are now extinct. There was a skeleton of a big 3-metre tall kangaroo and an enormous lion. These fossils tell us what Ice-Age animals were like in Australia over 10,000 years ago.

Fossil skeletons of a lion (above) and a kangaroo (below).

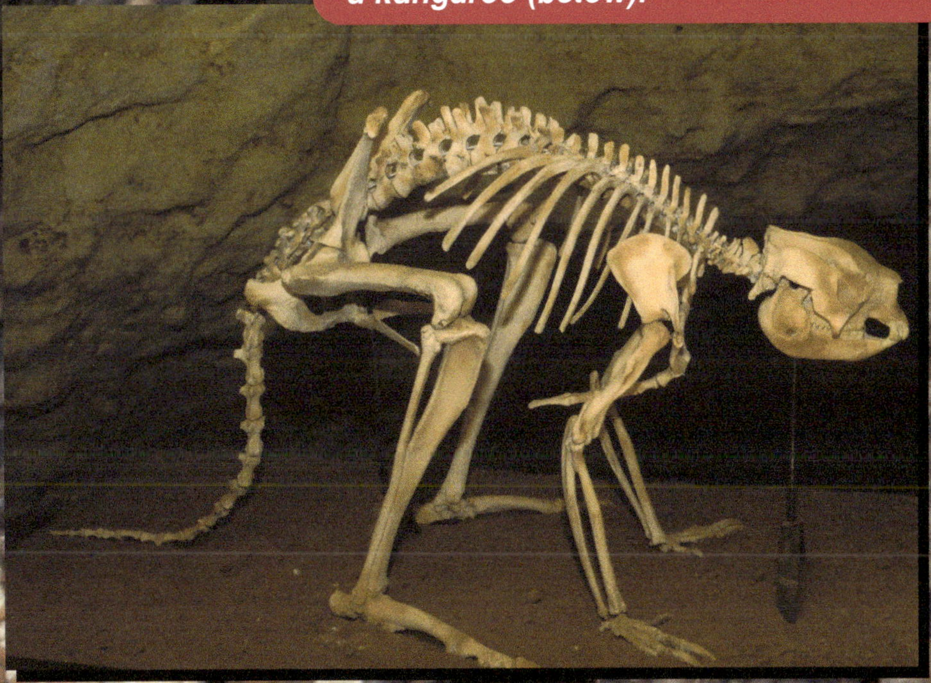

Living in caves

Prehistoric people sometimes lived in caves. All around the world, there are prehistoric cave paintings. Some of the cave paintings in France and Spain are more than 30,000 years old.

A cave painting in Altimira cave in Spain.

Man-made caves

In the past, people carved into rock and made caves. Sometimes they did this to escape from cold or hot weather. Sometimes they made caves to hide from their enemies.

In the 7th and 8th centuries in Cappadocia in Turkey, people carved enormous underground cities into the rocks. More than 20,000 people lived in different underground cities and they were safe from their enemies. The city of Derinkuyu has 18 underground floors and there are special tunnels to bring air into the caves.

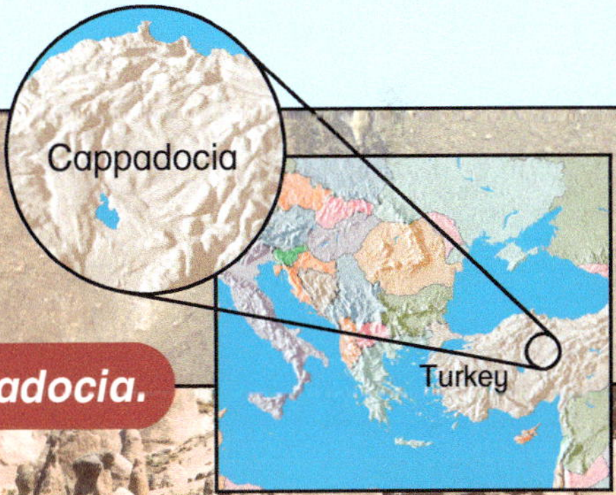

Entrances to caves in Cappadocia.

Modern caves

People still live in caves today. In Australia the temperature can be 60°C in summer. Many of the houses in the mining town of Coober Pedy are underground because it is cooler here.

An underground home in Coober Pedy.

Gopher holes at Coober Pedy.

Sacromonte in Granada in Spain is well known for its caves. People continue to live there today.

Did you know that ...

... if you want to live in a cave, you can buy a cave house on the Internet?

Exploring caves

People who explore caves for fun are called *cavers* or *potholers*.

Caving is an exciting hobby but it can be dangerous. Caves and passages are often very narrow and cavers have to crawl on hands and knees. Caves can be very high and cavers sometimes have to use ropes to climb up and down walls of rock.

Cavers need a hard hat with a light, strong boots, gloves and climbing equipment and ropes.

Caves are usually cold and wet, so cavers also need warm, comfortable clothes and protection for knees and elbows.

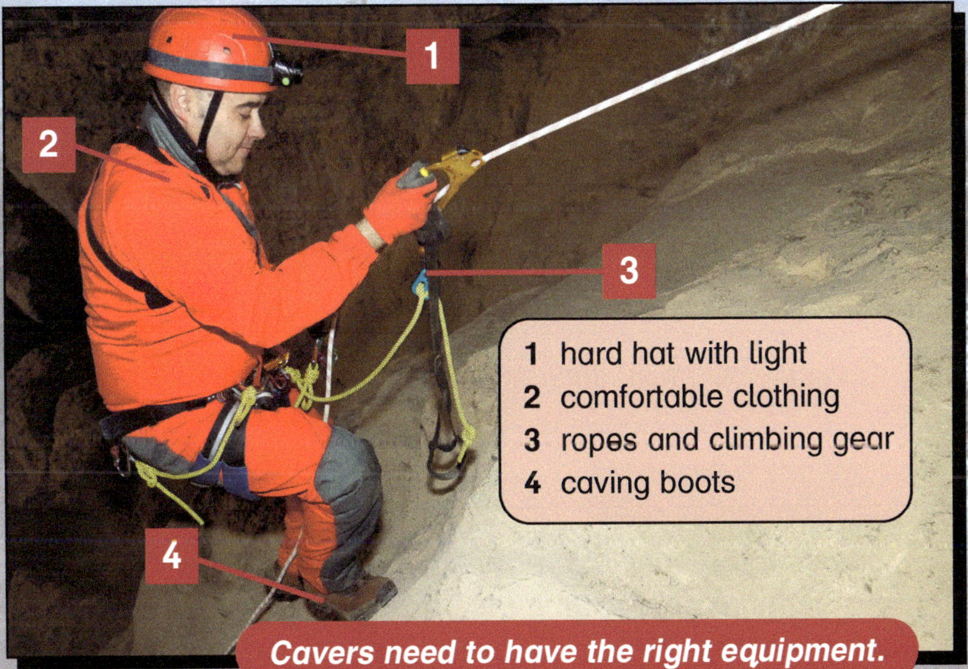

1 hard hat with light
2 comfortable clothing
3 ropes and climbing gear
4 caving boots

Cavers need to have the right equipment.

Safe caving

When cavers go exploring, they always go with a group of people. Each caver takes three different lights.

For underwater caves, cavers need diving equipment and rubber boots.

Do you hate small, dark places? If so, don't go caving!

Did you know that ...

... cavers learn special breathing exercises and movements to help them if they are trapped in a narrow passage?

The Lucky Accident

Written by Meryl Wilford

Illustrated by Dave Thompson

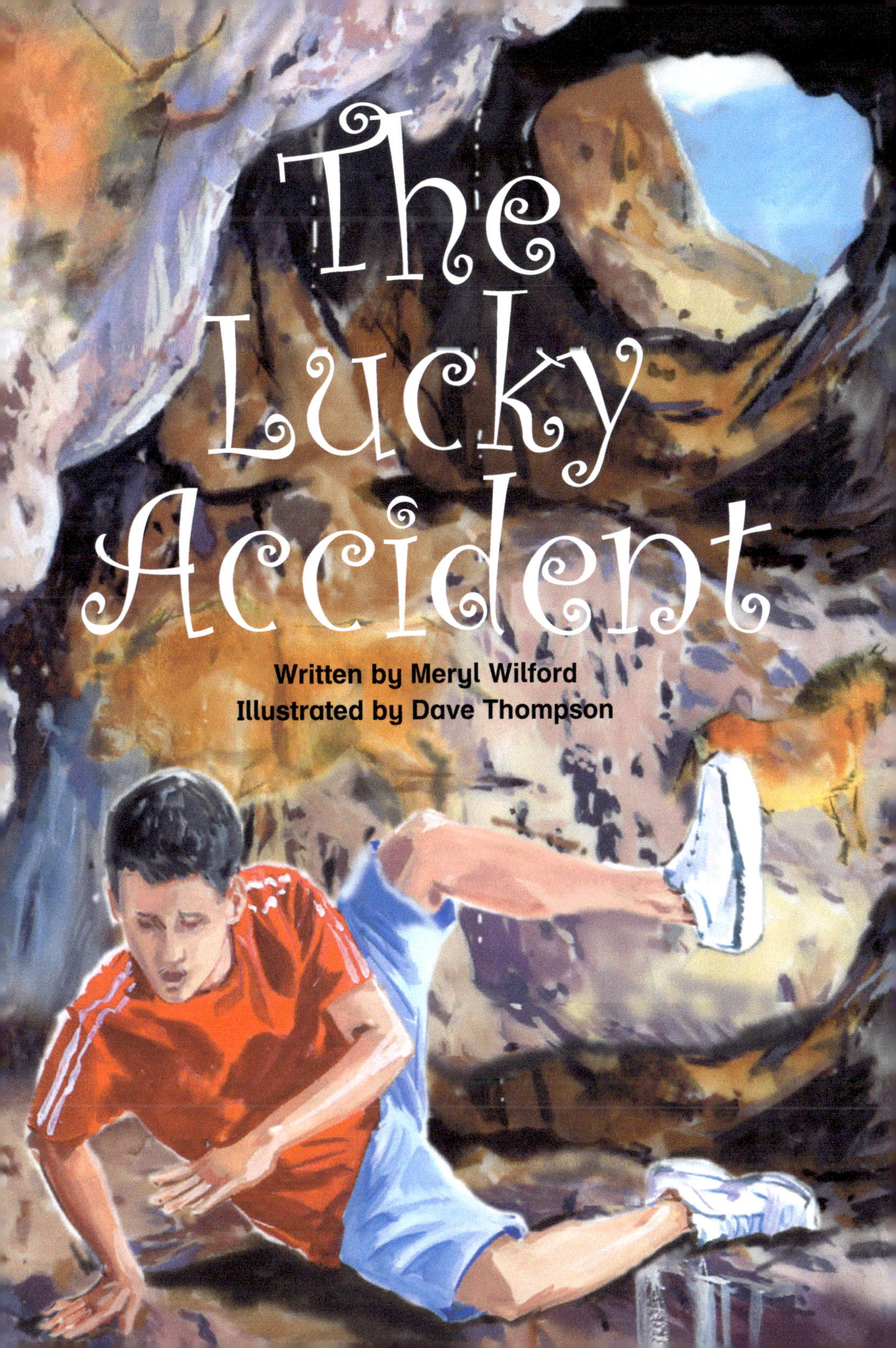

One very hot summer, David and Ruth went camping with their cousins, Sarah and Joe. After hours in the car, they arrived at the campsite and they helped their parents with the tents.
Who's got my sleeping bag?
This tent is cool.
What a great place.
I'm hungry.

Can we go for a walk up that hill?
OK. Take the water bottle.
And some biscuits!
See you later then. Bye.
See you later.

The cousins climbed the hill. It was hard work! At the top, they rested on some rocks and drank some water. Then they decided to play hide and seek.
I can see a good place to hide. Don't tell Sarah!
OK, I'm going to climb the tree.
I'm going to hide here.
One, two, three! I'm coming, ready or not.

David discovered a great hiding place between two big rocks. He stayed there and waited.
Suddenly he heard Sarah's voice. He moved back a little … then a little more, and a little bit more and ... and then he started to roll over and over.
Ahhh ... ouch ... my arm ... ... help ... help ... HELP!!

Everyone stopped the game and ran towards the rocks. Sarah started to cry.
Are you OK? David, say something!
Oh no, your Mum and Dad are going to be angry!
What are we going to do now? David, can you hear us?
I'm OK. A bit dirty ... don't worry! But how am I going to get out of here? It's very dark. I can't see anything.
Don't worry. We are going to find someone who can help.

David ate the biscuit in his pocket but he was very cold and very hungry. The water went drip, drip, drip. His clothes were cold and wet. He didn´t feel happy. Suddenly he saw someone at the top of the hole.
OK David, we're here to help you. I'm going to put a bag on a rope for you. It's coming down now!

The bag banged against the rock as it went down the hole. A rope touched David's arm. He looked in the bag.
Great! A jumper, a bottle of water, some biscuits and a torch. Thanks!
We are going to come down now. What's it like down there?

David used the torch to look at the walls of the cave. The cave was bigger than he imagined and he looked carefully at the walls and ceiling.

There was a long silence as David moved the light over the wall.
There are some animals. There are deer, I think, and some buffalo. But I can't see very well. Hurry up!

Latest edition

INCREDIBLE NEW CAVE DISCOVERY

FOUR CHILDREN made an amazing discovery last week. A cave with cave paintings more than 20,000 years old!

The children were on a camping holiday in the north of Spain. They discovered the cave by accident.

"This is amazing! Something like this can only happen once in a lifetime," said one of the scientists who visited the cave.

Activities

1 Circle T (True) or F (False)

1	The Carlsbad Caves are the biggest cave system in the world.	T	F
2	There is a cave with fossil skeletons of giant lions in Kenya.	T	F
3	Stalactites grow down from the roof of caves.	T	F
4	The Ozark cave fish has no eyes and no colour.	T	F
5	The longest lava cave is more than 30 kilometres long.	T	F
6	Derinkuyu is an underground city in Australia.	T	F
7	Ice caves are not very dangerous.	T	F
8	Some cave paintings are more than 30,000 years old.	T	F

2 Find the names of the nine animals mentioned in the book.

s	c	o	r	p	i	o	n	s
c	a	k	a	t	l	s	x	u
b	b	a	t	g	i	b	c	w
u	p	n	e	n	t	s	i	r
f	l	g	m	r	f	p	k	n
f	c	a	v	e	f	i	s	h
a	p	r	y	e	a	d	y	v
l	i	o	n	l	d	e	e	r
o	i	o	u	r	b	r	f	c
g	b	u	f	k	i	t	n	e

3 Read and match.

1	Bears use caves	sea caves.
2	You can find ice caves	about Ice-Age animals.
3	Most caves are in	under glaciers.
4	Volcanoes sometimes make	live underground.
5	The sea cuts into cliffs and makes	to sleep in winter.
6	Caving is a	limestone rock.
7	Many people in Coober Pedy	dangerous hobby.
8	Fossil skeletons tell us	lava caves.

4 Label the diagram of the cave and the potholer.

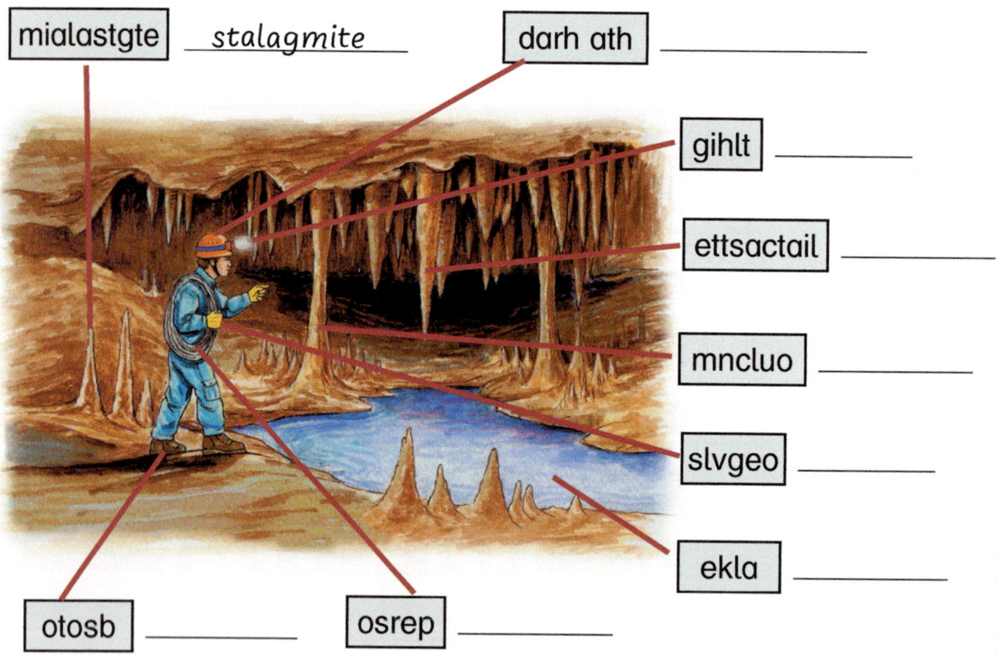

5 **Match the objects with the children or with the cavers.**

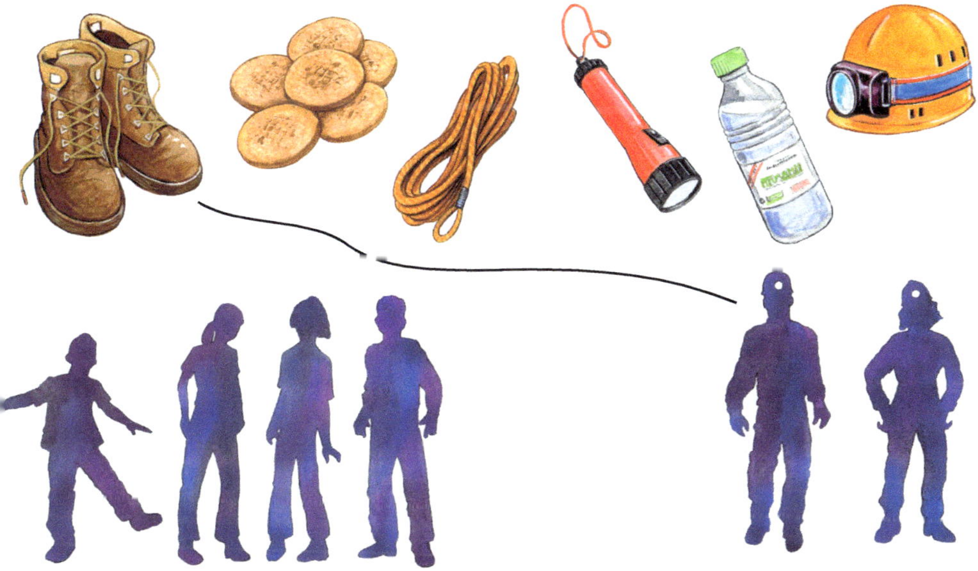

6 **Here is a postcard that Ruth sent to a friend. Circle the correct words.**

Hi Diana

We are having a (great / boring) time.

The weather is (rainy / hot) and we go to the beach every day.

We are staying in a (tent / hotel).

My (sister / brother) David had an accident. He is (ill / fine) now.

We found some (paintings/fossils).

They (is/are) amazing!

See you soon

Lots of love

Ruth

Diana Brown
8 Tall Trees Road
Burnley
BUR XP3 9QZ
ENGLAND

7 A friend is asking David about his holiday. Order and write the questions.

1 at / Did / a / you / stay / hotel? Did you stay at a hotel?
David: No, we stayed at a campsite.

2 with / were / Who / you? ______
David: I was with my cousins.

3 an / Did / you / have / accident? ______
David: Yes, I did. But I was OK.

4 wet / Was / the / cave? ______
David: Yes, it was very wet and very dark.

5 see / did / the / What / cave / you / in? ______
David: I saw paintings on the walls.

6 like / you / Do / caves? ______
David: Yes, I do. I want to be a caver when I'm older.

8 Write about this cave. Look at the picture and answer these questions:

1 Where is this cave? ______

2 Who lives in the cave? ______

3 What is the boy going to do? ______

______

Bilingual Dictionary

Write the words in your language.

accident ____________
appear ____________
bear ____________
blind ____________
buffalo ____________
carve ____________
cave ____________
caver ____________
chimney ____________
cliff ____________
connect ____________
cool ____________
cover ____________
crack ____________
crawl ____________
dangerous ____________
darkness ____________
discovery ____________
dissolve ____________
elbow ____________
enemy ____________
equipment ____________
erupt ____________
extinct ____________
formation ____________
fossil ____________
freeze ____________
glacier ____________
grow ____________
hard ____________
hide ____________
hobby ____________
hole ____________
ice ____________
Ice-Age ____________
kangeroo ____________
lava ____________
limestone ____________
melt ____________
mining ____________
narrow ____________
passage ____________
potholer ____________
protection ____________
rainwater ____________
rope ____________
safe ____________
scorpion ____________
skeleton ____________
soft ____________
stalactite ____________
stalagmite ____________
survive ____________
torch ____________
tube ____________
tunnel ____________
underground ____________

Macmillan Education
4 Crinan Street
London N1 9XW
A division of Springer Nature Limited
Companies and representatives throughout the world

ISBN 978-1-3800-3770-1

First published 2005
This edition published 2019

Illustrated by Dave Thompson/Beehive Illustration
Designed by Marion James Design

The authors and publishers would like to thank the following for permission to reproduce their photographs:

Cover image by gettyimages/JCMarcos

Title page image by Getty Images/Marc Dufresne

Auscape International p4 ©Dennis Harding, 8 ©Reg Morrison, Alamy Stock Photo/BIOSPHOTO 10, 11(t), Getty Images/Marc Dozier 14(t, m), ©Andy Belcher, 16(b) ©Kevin Beacon; Alamy/Cavan Images/Alamy Stock Photo p9, 12, 13; Getty Images/EyeEm/Steven Swinnen p5, Getty Images/iStockphoto/PEDRE p13; Getty Images/iStock/pedrosala p15, Getty Images/E+/simonkr p16(tr); Karora/Wikimedia p11(b); Robert Harding Picture Library p3; Alamy Stock Photo/Nature Picture Library p10, Getty Images/estivillml p14(b).

Printed and bound in Brazil

2025
7